THE PYRAMID BUILDERS

Turning Points in World History

THE PYRAMID BUILDERS

Carter Smith III

Silver Burdett Press, Inc.

Acknowledgments

The author and editor thank Ronald Sheridan of the Ancient Art and Architecture Collection and John E. Rosenthal of Rosenthal Art Slides for their invaluable help in text and picture research.

Consultants

We thank the following people for reviewing the manuscript and offering their helpful suggestions:

Robert M. Goldberg
Consultant to the Social Studies Department
  (formerly Department Chair)
Oceanside Middle School
Oceanside, New York

Loy Fook Lee
Master of Architecture Degree
Columbia University

Cover: The Great Pyramid at Giza with the Sphinx in the foreground. Courtesy of Woodfin Camp & Associates.

Title Page: A panoramic view of the pyramids at Giza, just outside the modern Egyptian capital of Cairo. Courtesy of the Bettmann Archive.

Contents Page: One of the pyramids at Giza was built for the Old Kingdom pharaoh Menkaure, shown here with his queen, Khamer-Ernesty. Courtesy of Rosenthal Art Slides.

Back Cover: A page from The Book of the Dead, Ancient Egypt's most sacred religious text. Courtesy of the Mary Evans Picture Library.

Library of Congress Cataloging-in-Publication Data

Smith, Carter.
The pyramid builders / Carter Smith III.
    p.   cm. — (Turning points in world history)
Includes bibliographical references and index.
Summary: Describes the construction of the pyramids and the
religious, cultural, and political traditions of ancient Egypt.
    1. Egypt — History — To 332 B.C. — Juvenile literature. [1. Egypt-
- History — To 332 B.C. 2. Pyramids.] I. Title. II. Series.
DT83.S64   1991
932--dc20
                                                        90-26022
                                                        CIP
                                                        AC

Editorial Coordination by Richard G. Gallin

 Created by Media Projects Incorporated

Carter Smith, *Executive Editor*
Charles A. Wills, *Series Editor*
Bernard Schleifer, *Design Consultant*
Paul Pugliese, *Cartographer*

Manufactured in the United States of America.

ISBN   0-382-24131-2 [lib. bdg.]
10 9 8 7 6 5 4 3 2 1

ISBN   0-382-24137-1 [pbk.]
10 9 8 7 6 5 4 3 2 1

CONTENTS

Introduction
THE MYSTERY OF THE PYRAMIDS   7

1   **THE SEEDS OF CIVILIZATION**   11

2   **EGYPT ASCENDANT**   17

3   **THE TRIUMPH OF THEBES**   39

4   **THE DECLINE OF AN EMPIRE**   53

Afterword
REDISCOVERING ANCIENT EGYPT   57

Index   62

Suggested Reading   64

The Mystery of the Pyramids

In about the year 2470 B.C., Sahure, the pharaoh (king) of Egypt, died. Although his people grieved for their ruler, they believed his soul would live forever.

Long before Sahure died, the people of Egypt had prepared to protect his body from the weather and from thieves who might try to steal the riches that would be placed in their king's tomb. They also believed that the king's spirit would need a home where it could spend eternity. During Sahure's lifetime, much of Egypt's population worked to build him a special tomb at the edge of the desert. The tomb, built in the shape of a pyramid, was joined to the Nile River by a road called a causeway.

Just after Sahure died, his body was taken to a workshop on the west bank of the Nile. There, Sahure's body was mummified—preserved. While Sahure was being mummified, workmen con-

The Pyramid of Khufu (Cheops) at Giza is the largest of Egypt's pyramids.

structed his coffins. Three different coffins were built, each fitting inside the other. Each coffin was painted with religious symbols. Finally, all three coffins were put inside a large outer coffin called a sarcophagus.

On the day of Sahure's burial, boats carried his mummy along the Nile to his tomb. Accompanying the king's body were several attendants, his coffin, and the possessions—furniture, clothes, and other belongings—that he would use in the afterlife.

After landing, the mummy was placed in a booth-shaped shrine and covered with flowers. This shrine was placed on a frame called a bier, which was pulled to the temple of Sahure's tomb by oxen. In front of the oxen walked a priest, waving a wand called a censer. Sahure's family and important guests followed the mummy. Behind them, on a small sled, came the jars holding the pharaoh's internal organs.

Once the funeral procession reached the tomb, the priests performed religious ceremonies. The most important ceremony was called the Opening of the Mouth, which returned to the mummy all of the functions that it had lost when the pharaoh died. The priests performed other rituals to help Sahure's spirit sail to the skies, where he would join Re, the god of the sun. Meanwhile, a new king took Sahure's place as ruler of the land of the living. Soon, the Egyptian people would begin work on the new ruler's pyramid.

Although almost 4,500 years have passed since the day King Sahure died, historians know a surprising amount about his people. Much of what we know about Egyptian history comes from the writings of an Egyptian priest named Manetho. Manetho divided his country's history into "dynasties," with each dynasty of pharaohs usually coming from the same family. New dynasties began when a different family of pharaohs took over the throne. In all, thirty-one different dynasties ruled over Egypt. Modern historians have divided it up even further, into several phases. The main ones are the Old Kingdom, the Middle Kingdom, and the New Kingdom. Sahure lived during what is known as the Fifth Dynasty, which ruled during the Old Kingdom.

Ancient Egypt's civilization lasted almost three thousand years, far longer than any other the world has ever seen. If the entire history of the United States were to repeat itself ten times over, it would still be much shorter than that of ancient Egypt. In fact, when the ancient Greek historian Herodotus visited Egypt almost twenty-five centuries ago

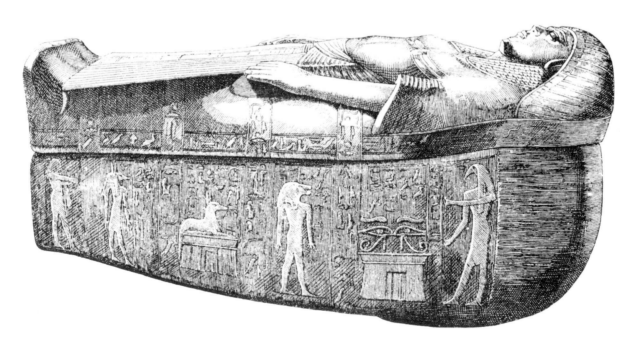

A pharaoh's mummified body was placed in a sarcophagus, like the one here before burial.

and described "wonders more in number than those of any other land," Egypt was as old to him then as he is to us now.

Today, travelers in Egypt can view many of the same wonders that Herodotus did. The pyramids of the Old Kingdom period, where the bodies of the pharaohs were buried, still symbolize Egyptian civilization more than any other monuments. Sahure's pyramid, which still stands near the town of Abusir, has unfortunately been damaged over time. Better known are the awe-inspiring pyramids at Giza, outside the modern nation of Egypt's capital city of Cairo. Built for the Fourth Dynasty kings Khufu, Khafre, and Menkaure (or Cheops, Chephren, and Mycerinus, as Herodotus named them), these pyramids are perhaps the most famous symbols of ancient civilization anywhere in the world.

The oldest and tallest of the three is the pyramid built for Cheops, known as the Great Pyramid, which was completed around 2650 B.C. The Great Pyramid is built of over two million blocks of limestone, each weighing up to fifteen tons.

Near Cheops' Great Pyramid is the pyramid built for his son Chephren. Although it appears taller than the Great Pyramid, it is merely built on higher ground and at a steeper angle. Just below Chephren's pyramid stands the strange limestone beast that the Greeks named the Great Sphinx. The giant figure has the body of a lion 240 feet long and 66 feet high and a human being's face that measures over 13 feet across.

Many historians believe that the face is that of Chephren himself.

Although archaeologists have uncovered much information about ancient Egypt, these great monuments remain shrouded in mystery. No exact record of how the pyramids and the Sphinx were built exists, but we do know that only a highly organized, sophisticated, and united society could have built them. Other civiliations developed before ancient Egypt, but Egpyptian society attained a kind of order and stability that was largely unknown to other ancient civilizations.

Even though their ancient monuments of stone tell of a people long vanished, the Egyptian people were a living, breathing society. Their discoveries and contributions changed the course of human history and remain with us today. It was the Egyptians who invented the first calendar based on the sun's movements, who developed the hieroglyphic alphabet (a system of writing based on pictures), who created the first system of bringing water to dry lands, and who created the first written study on surgery. These are only a few of the Egyptian contributions that give life to the record left by the pyramids. Although Sahure's pyramid and most others have been ravaged by time and raided by looters, they have served their purposes well. It is through them that we can look back over thousands of years to the land of the pharaohs. It is through them that the spirit of the pyramid builders continues to thrive some five thousand years later.

CHAPTER ONE

The Seeds of Civilization

"Hail to thee, O Nile, that issues from the earth and comes to keep Egypt alive . . ." So begins an Egyptian hymn to the Nile, the majestic river that stretches four thousand miles through the African continent—from mountain rain forests, through the Sahara, and finally into the Mediterranean Sea. To the ancient Egyptians, the Nile was a life-giving gift without which they could never have survived. The Nile itself is probably the single most important reason that a civilization as sophisticated and vital as theirs could have thrived for three thousand years.

The Nile creates a thin green strip of arable land (land suitable for farming) as it flows through the desert. In the north, the river fans out into many branches, or a delta, before it reaches the Mediterranean. This part of Egypt was called Lower Egypt. To the south,

This patch of land along the Nile looks much the way it did in the age of the pyramid builders.

where cliffs overhang the river's edge and farmland is more scarce, is Upper Egypt.

The strip watered by the Nile is only about thirteen miles wide, but it contains some of the most fertile land on earth. This is because of the Nile's yearly floods, which carry with them rich soil. It is in the Nile itself that the seeds of ancient Egypt's civilization can be found.

When the last ice age ended more than ten thousand years ago, much of the land that had been covered with grass dried up, becoming desert. Because the people and animals of the area needed water to survive, many moved into the green valley along the Nile.

These early people were nomads, which means that they constantly moved from place to place in search of food. By about 5000 B.C., however, they had discovered just how good the land of the Nile Valley was, and they began to gather the wild crops that grew along the river's banks. In time, they began to

This sketch, made from an Egyptian tomb painting, shows a peasant drawing water from the life-giving Nile with a shaduf. Irrigation was vital to ancient Egyptian agriculture.

plant and harvest crops like barley, wheat, and flax.

As the former nomads became accustomed to growing food instead of simply gathering it, they settled permanently in small villages. Their early houses were simple ones, made largely of mud bricks dried by the sun.

As rich as the Nile's bounty has been, as recently as a century ago Egyptians depended on the annual floods to bring them the soil necessary for planting. The people never knew how big the flood would be from year to year. Some years, the flood might bring too much water and not enough soil; the next year might bring a drought. To cultivate as much farmland as possible to feed the growing village populations, the early Egyptians developed a system of irrigation. They dug canals to bring water to the land on either bank of the Nile. To guide the water from the Nile into these canals, they devised a simple water hoist called a *shaduf*. It consisted of a long pole balanced on a crossbeam. On one end of the pole was a rope with a bucket tied to the end. On the other end was a heavy weight. By pulling the rope, workers could lower the bucket into the Nile. The weight would then raise the bucket and lift the water into the ditch.

Some Egyptian farmers use shadufs even today.

Besides regulating the annual floods through irrigation, the people of the Nile had other concerns. Those villagers whose land bore a particular type of fruit that other tribes wanted, for example, had something to protect. Because towns with large populations had more people to defend them, the early Egyptians saw fertility—the ability to grow healthy crops and have a bigger population—as a supreme good. Many villages had animals that symbolized certain qualities of fertility.

For these early Egyptians, control over nature also meant control over human enemies. Whoever could command the largest tribe, or arm themselves with the best weapons, could protect themselves from attack and control a village or even a group of villages.

As more and more villages grew up along the Nile, some naturally became stronger than others. The smaller communities began to look to the larger ones for protection. Eventually, groups of villages began to band together into districts called *nomes*.

The most dramatic event in this earliest period of Egyptian history is illustrated by a carved stone slab, or palette, now housed in a Cairo museum. The palette illustrates what later Egyptians considered the starting point of their history—the unification of Upper and Lower Egypt into one nation. This was accomplished around 3100 B.C. by Narmer, the chief of a powerful southern tribe.

According to Herodotus and to Egyptian legend, the first king of Egypt was named Menes. The legend claims that Menes "raised the dike which protects Memphis from the inundations [floods] of the Nile." Many experts believe that Menes and Narmer are the same person. They argue that all kings of Egypt had five names, and that Narmer must simply be another name for Menes.

Whatever the answer is to this mystery, the Narmer Palette, as it is called, was an important and fascinating discovery. The palette illustrates the unification of Egypt through pictures, making it perhaps the first written record of a historic event. On one side of the palette, the king is shown wearing the cone-shaped crown of Upper Egypt and clubbing a helpless enemy into defeat. To the right of this scene is the falcon-god Horus, who represents the king. Horus is perching triumphantly over a papyrus plant that represents the defeated Lower Egypt. On the palette's other side, Narmer is wearing the red crown of Lower Egypt. He is shown standing in front of the bodies of ten of his enemies, whose heads have all been chopped off and neatly placed between their legs.

Judging from that scene, Narmer must have united Upper and Lower Egypt through war. Another scene on the palette shows that he made peace with his enemy. Two giant monsters, with lion's faces and giraffe-like necks, are shown with necks intertwined, symbolizing the union of two equals.

After uniting the nation, Narmer, or

One side of the Narmer Palette depicts Menes, or Narmer, subduing Lower Egypt.

The reverse side of the Narmer Palette uses two giant beasts with intertwined necks to symbolize the unification of Upper and Lower Egypt.

Menes, founded the first of what would be thirty-one dynasties, and built his capital at Memphis, a town just south of the Nile delta. During the three hundred years between his reign and the first rulers of the Old Kingdom, the groundwork was laid for the growing state of Egypt. The country eventually became a rich one. To govern this growing country, Menes and the other pharaohs of the First and Second Dynasties saw to it that their laws were obeyed by all. He and his successors ruled for about four hundred years, or from about 3100 to 2686 B.C. The stage was set for Egypt's greatest period of glory and power, the Old Kingdom. The era of the pyramid builders was about to begin.

CHAPTER TWO

Egypt Ascendant

Soon after Menes united Upper and Lower Egypt, the people of the Nile began to see themselves as a specially chosen people living in a paradise on earth. So comfortable were the Egyptians with their fate that they saw little reason to change the way they lived. In fact, from the founding of a united Egypt in 3100 B.C. to the last pharaoh of the Thirtieth Dynasty, Egyptian society stayed much the same.

By the year 2686 B.C.—the first year of what is called the Old Kingdom—the rulers had already brought order and stability to Egyptian society. Local rulers had lost their independence to the pharaohs, whose control over every part of life was total.

The pharaoh was not simply the country's most powerful politician. He was thought to be a god who would return to heaven after death. The fate of the people was in his hands. Following

This statue of the pharaoh Zoser is seen through an opening in his tomb, the famous step pyramid designed by his chief architect, Imhotep, at Saqqara.

his laws was not only a legal obligation but a religious one as well. "If you want to know what to do in life," wrote one Egyptian, "cling to the pharaoh and be loyal."

By the time of the Old Kingdom, the pharaoh was thought to maintain the *Ma'at*, or the natural order of the universe. Since he has considered a god, all land was his and all Egyptians were his servants.

One helpful way to look at Egyptian society is to look at it as if it was shaped like a pyramid. At the very top was the pharaoh. Beneath the pharaoh was the upper class, or aristocracy. Among this group were the priests and nobles of the pharaoh's court. On the next level came the middle class, made up of merchants and craftspeople. The lower class, which was by far the largest, was made up of peasants, laborers, and slaves.

Although all law came from the pharaoh, he didn't rule without help. His chief assistant, the vizier, acted as overseer of the nomes (provinces), supervisor of all government departments, and

An Old Kingdom statue depicts a scribe with a clay tablet and a writing instrument.

chief adviser to the pharaoh. The pharaoh also had a treasurer, a minister of public works, and a commander-in-chief of the military. Finally, different regions of the country were ruled by governors.

Priests were among the most important people in Egyptian society. Besides performing daily ceremonies and annual festivals to the gods of their temples, they made predictions and said special prayers in exchange for money or other payment.

Between the upper and middle classes were the scribes, who were responsible for keeping written records. Scribes were highly educated because they needed to master the elaborate hiero-

glyphic alphabet. Their education took place in the temples, where they also learned mathematics, architecture, medicine, and law. Artists, too, were valued members of Egyptian society, and several court artists were given handsome tombs by their pharaohs.

The lower classes of Egyptian society were mostly uneducated and at the mercy of the higher classes. Sometimes they were ordered to work on irrigation projects or to haul the huge stones used for pyramid building.

Much of our knowledge of the role of women in Egyptian society comes from decorations in tombs. The most important role of the Egyptian woman seems to have been as wife and mother. In many tomb paintings, the wife of the tomb owner is elegantly dressed and sits with her husband. Sometimes she is shown accompanying her husband as he watches scenes of work. Most often, however, she is depicted indoors, inside the home.

It seems likely that the women depicted this way are the wives of wealthy men. Since the husbands are shown watching others work, and not working themselves, they are probably members of the aristocracy.

Women of the lower classes mostly worked indoors, too. Many tomb paintings show women baking bread, brewing beer, or weaving garments. The color of female skin is also painted lighter than male skin on the tomb decorations, which probably means that women were not in the sun as often as men. In fact, straying far from the

THE EGYPTIAN GODS

A statue of Osiris.

The Egyptians worshiped many different gods, and learning about them all can be a complicated and confusing process. Egyptian religion often seems like a series of contradictions. Originally, the Egyptians worshiped gods representing the forces of nature that affected them every day—the sun, for example. Many animals, like lions and crocodiles, were also considered gods.

In time, the Egyptians gave gods human qualities and forms, although some gods kept their animal heads. Each region had its own gods, and a few were prayed to by all. Each god also had a story behind it, but many of the stories changed over the years. According to one story, for example, the world was originally just water until the sun god (originally called Atum, and later called Re) arose on a mound of land. He created the gods of air and moisture. Their daughter was named Nut, the goddess of the sky. Nut was portrayed as a woman whose body curved across the sky. Her brother, Geb, was god of the earth, and also her husband. Together Geb and Nut had four children. The first, Osiris, represented by a dead king, was god of the underworld. Osiris, called "the perfect one," was one of the most important and best-loved gods. His brother, Seth—god of the desert, storms, and violence—murdered him, cutting his body up and scattering it across the country. Osiris' wife and sister, together with his sister Nephthys, found the pieces and put him back together.

The goddess Isis was especially important to the pharaohs. After she had brought back Osiris from the dead, she gave birth to Horus, the heavenly falcon, who represented the living pharaoh. According to the legend, when he became old enough, Horus got revenge on Seth by overcoming him in battle.

Another god that is especially important is Amun, the god of Thebes, who in time became the chief god of all Egypt. He was closely identified with the sun god, Re, and was sometimes called Amun-Re.

home may have been dangerous for women in ancient Egypt. According to one text, the pharaoh Ramses III, who ruled during the new Kingdom period (1567–1085 B.C.), "enabled the woman of Egypt to go her way, her journeys being extended where she wanted, without any other person assaulting her on the road."

Few women held important jobs except for a few female priests, and apart from members of the royal family and ruling queens, they had little political power. In fact, most women could not read or write and therefore were unable to join the government. Age and wisdom were not even considered to be desirable qualities in women. In tomb paintings, the dead man's mother often looks identical to his wife.

Since much of what we know about Egyptian women has been found inside the tombs of Egyptian men, we only know how men saw them and not necessarily how they really were. In reality, the Egyptian woman's influence may have been greater than what we can tell from the evidence we have.

To the typical Egyptian of either sex, one's place in society was beyond control. Because the pharaoh protected the "established order of the Universe," every citizen of Egypt had his or her place in it according to these laws.

Religion affected much more than the role of women or even the role of the pharaoh in society. The pharaoh was one of the most important gods, but certainly not the only one. Historians have counted over two thousand different

Egyptian gods, spirits, and demons. Many were only worshiped in certain regions or towns, while others were revered throughout the land. Some gods were minor at one time but grew in importance. For example, Osiris began as the local god of the Nile Delta. Over time, Osiris became so important in Egyptian religion that a pharaoh's people believed that when he died he became Osiris.

Egyptian tomb sites featured elaborate complexes of temples. The one pictured here is at Saqqara.

During the Old Kingdom, Egyptians believed that life after death was reserved for the pharaoh, his family, and the nobility. They also felt that even after passing from the earth, the dead king had the same influence over events as the new living king. They believed that after death, the dead king's *ka*, or spiritual double, would live on in his corpse. Since the ka took time to develop, it was important that the phar-aoh's body not be disturbed. And because the underworld where the dead king lived was seen as the other half of existence, the ka would have the same needs that the living king did on earth. For that reason, a pharaoh's tomb was equipped with many of the things that he had used in life. If the king had been fed the finest food and drink on earth, for example, his ka would certainly need the same.

The Egyptians also believed that the pharaoh's ka required a home that would last forever. The pharaoh would need much more that a simple grave. Instead, he would need an entire complex with many different buildings surrounded by walls to keep out intruders. At the center of this walled complex was the pharaoh's tomb. By the Fourth Dynasty, the pharaoh's tomb had evolved into what we know today as the pyramids.

The pyramids, however, were only the centerpiece of the complex. In front of the pyramid was a temple, known as the mortuary temple, in which funeral ceremonies were performed by the pharaoh's priests. There would also be buildings for sacrificing animals in tribute to the pharaoh and warehouses for storing his treasures. The tombs of the king's family and court were also located within the complex, so that they would be close by if the pharaoh needed them in the afterlife.

These complexes, often called funerary districts, were more than just cemeteries. To the Egyptians, a funerary district was an alternate world. It was the world of the dead, where the ka of the dead pharaohs lived out eternity. Funerary districts were always just beyond the west bank of the Nile, since that was where the sun set at the end of each day.

That the king's funeral complexes developed into immense structures had little to do with the ego of any one pharaoh. It had more to do with making sure the pharaoh's life would be eternal. If his ka could survive forever, the pharaoh could continue to bless his people with divine wisdom.

A particular pharaoh's tomb can tell a lot about the state of Egyptian society during his lifetime, even from the earliest days of Egypt. There are many signs that even after Menes united the two Egypts, a power struggle between the two regions continued. Historians believe this because some First and Second Dynasty pharaohs were buried in the north, at Saqqara, and others were buried in the south, at Abydos. Although little else is known about these rulers, we know that they were not buried in pyramids. Instead, they were buried in long, rectangular, flat-topped brick tombs called *mastabas*, which is the modern Arabic word for "benches." A mastaba was made of dried mud bricks, and the structures resemble the benches that stand outside Egyptian houses.

The First and Second Dynasty Egyptians decorated their mastabas by arranging the bricks in different patterns. Inside, often below the ground, were several burial chambers—one for the pharaoh's body and the others for the possessions or treasures left with the corpse. In time, mastabas grew bigger, some as tall as 17 feet. Eventually they began to be built with fancier materials. One First Dynasty pharaoh had the floor of his burial pit laid with limestone from the nearby hills. Eventually, some pharaohs built mastabas with as many as thirty chambers.

History is full of people and events that seem to burst onto the scene and change the course of things to come.

A later sketch of the flat-topped brick tombs, called mastabas, *which were in use before the Ancient Egyptians began building pyramids. The largest concentrations of mastabas are at Abydos and Saqqara.*

Imhotep, the personal architect of the pharaoh Zoser, was this kind of person. Zoser was the first ruler anywhere to employ an architect so talented that his name lives on to this day. During Zoser's Third Dynasty reign, which lasted from about 2686 to 2613 B.C., Imhotep built his king the most elaborate tomb yet seen in Egypt. Imhotep's work on the tomb was so advanced that he was considered a genius during his own lifetime. Like the pharaoh, he was worshiped as a god for centuries after his death.

Zoser was buried in the funerary district outside Memphis at Saqqara. His tomb was surrounded by a protective wall and contained a gigantic monument built of small stone blocks, instead of the mud bricks used on mastabas. The stones formed six square platforms, one on top of the next, forming a great step pyramid just over 200 feet high. (A step pyramid is a pyramid built in layers that grow narrower as they rise.) Zoser's funeral complex also contained a temple where offerings could be made.

Even today, archaeologists are impressed with Imhotep's achievements. While building Zoser's step pyramid, he continually made changes to improve the structure. First, he decided to build a mastaba that was square instead of rectangular. His second innovation was to change the building material. In mastabas from the First and Second Dynasties, stones were only used for floors and

A statue of Imhotep, chief architect of the pharaoh Zoser and one of Ancient Egypt's greatest builders.

sometimes for doorways. Imhotep decided that he would use a core of limestone on the tomb and surround it with an outer shell of stone. Eventually he had built a square mastaba that was 26 feet high with 207-foot-long sides.

Imhotep, however, was still not satisfied. He decided to extended the square by 14 feet on each side, at a height 2 feet lower than the original mastaba. Now he had a two-step structure.

The two-step mastaba may have given him the idea to continue enlarging the first level and then put three more levels on top of the base. He now had a four-step pyramid. Imhotep still wasn't satisfied. His final pyramid was six levels high, rising over 200 feet above the desert floor.

The sheer size of Zoser's step pyramid and the methods he used to build it had never been seen in Egypt before. Imhotep pioneered the techniques that would give birth to one of the greatest periods of building that humankind has ever known.

At Maidum, in central Egypt, is a pyramid that may give a clue about how the Egyptians moved from step-pyramids to the first true pyramids. This is a tower-like structure that stands above a hill of stone rubble. This structure is all that remains of the first true pyramid ever attempted.

Historians are not sure whether this pyramid was built for Huni, the last pharoah of the Third Dynasty, or for Snefru, the first Fourth Dynasty ruler. In any case, the monument started out as a seven-step pyramid, but an eighth

The lower level of Zoser's step pyramid, showing the ventilation shafts sunk into the structure's base.

step was added. Once that was complete, the builders filled in the steps and added an outer casing. This gave the structure its form as a true, slope-sided pyramid.

Unfortunately, the outer casing of the pyramid collapsed during construction. Worse, the outer casing didn't rest on a firm foundation, and the blocks that it was made out of were not positioned correctly. These mistakes caused the four outer walls of the pyramid to collapse, leaving only the step tower that we see today.

The next attempt at building a true pyramid was more successful. Within a hundred years of Zoser's reign, one of his relatives, Queen Hetep-Heres, married Snefru, the first pharaoh of the Fourth Dynasty. While he may or may

not have built the fallen pyramid at Maidum, he was a tremendous builder. He built two different pyramids at Dashur, which is just south of Saqqara.

The most famous of Snefru's pyramids is the "bent" pyramid. It is called "bent" because when the structure reached more than half of its originally intended height the angle of the sloping sides was reduced sharply. This makes the pyramid look as if it is actually bent. The sides of Snefru's Bent Pyramid are curved—probably, say historians, because it had to be finished in a hurry. In the middle of construction, the angle of the sides was changed and the height was lowered. Lastly, the method of laying the casing and packing the pyramid's stone blocks was improved.

Another unusual characteristic of the

Modern Egyptians rest in the shade of the step pyramid at Saqqara.

Bent Pyramid is that it has two separate entrances, one in its northern face and another in the western face.

Snefru's second pyramid at Dashur is known as the "Red" or "Pink" pyramid because of the color of the limestone used to build it. Why Snofru built this second pyramid is unknown, but architects find it interesting that the angle of its slope is the same as on the upper part of the Bent Pyramid.

Why the Egyptians chose the true pyramid form at all for their tombs is a mystery. Some historians feel that the step pyramid built by Imhotep is similar to temples called ziggurats, which were built in Mesopotamia (now Iraq). Egyptians may have seen these stone monuments. Once they realized the possibility of building in stone, according to this

theory, they couldn't resist the temptation to build man-made mountains in the flat Egyptian landscape.

Others feel that the pyramid shape was simply a natural jump from Imhotep's step design. Since the Egyptians already had a strong knowledge of mathematics, the pure geometric shape of a pyramid was one that they probably found appealing.

A religious reason for the pyramid shape has also been suggested. Since he was seen as the god Horus, the pharaoh was also connected to the sun-god, Re. The pyramid shape resembles the rays of the sun as they often flare up in Egypt, and early religious writings describe how the king would use the sun's rays to climb up to heaven.

Finally, the pyramid shape may have

The "bent" pyramid built by the pharaoh Snefru at Dashur.

developed for a more simple and practical reason. Because the pyramid grows narrower as it rises, it requires progressively less material and labor as construction proceeds. Thus, the triangular pyramid shape might simply have been the most economical way of building a large-scale monument.

Partly because of these mysteries, the three pyramids that rise above the plateau at Giza have fascinated visitors throughout the ages. Both their enormous size and their perfectly symmetrical structures have awed archaeologists and tourists alike. We know they were built during the Fourth Dynasty (c. 2613–2498 B.C.), but exactly how they were built is still open to question. Clearly, the construction of a pyramid was a task that demanded a highly ad-

vanced level of organization. Each step of its construction was the result of a carefully chosen plan.

One of the greatest mysteries about the pyramids is how the Egyptians moved stones of such enormous weight without the help of the wheel. They left no written explanations. One theory is that the stones were slid along a surface of wet mud as if on a skating rink. It is an even greater mystery how they were able to raise each level of stone higher than the level before it. Some historians agree with the ancient Roman writer Diodorus Siculus, who lived during the first century B.C. He believed ramps were used to allow the laborers to drag stones up the slope of the pyramid. In fact, long before Cheops' lifetime, it seems probable that such ramps were in

THE MUMMY AND THE EGYPTIAN LAND OF THE DEAD

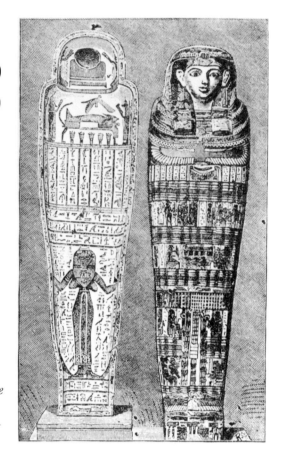

Two of the sarcophagi (coffins) into which the mummified bodies of pharaohs were placed.

One of the most famous symbols of ancient Egypt is the mummy. Surrounded by mystery, the mummy has been the subject of quite a bit of misunderstanding. Hollywood monster movies featuring mummies coming to life and stalking the earth for victims to devour are only one source of this confusion. The fact that Egyptians honored their dead by mummifying them has also led people to believe that the ancient Egyptians were obsessed with death. The opposite is true: Life was so fruitful and generally peaceful that they wanted to have it continue for eternity. The center of this belief lay in the *ka* and *ba* spirits contained in every body. The ka was the main force of life. Upon the body's physical death, the ka remained with the body in its tomb, caring for it for all time. The ba was symbolized by a human-headed bird, representing the particular personality of the deceased. During the day, the ba visited the world, and then it returned to the tomb at night. If the ka and ba were to survive, the Egyptians believed, the physical body had to be preserved. If the ka and ba did not survive, the afterlife of the dead person would end.

At first, the Egyptian dead were buried in the sand. Because the hot sand dried out bodies before they decomposed, they could be preserved naturally this way. Gradually, more elaborate tombs were built. Because the bodies were no longer preserved by sand, different methods were used to keep them intact.

The first method of mummification involved wrapping the body with resin-coated bandages and then painting a portrait of the person's face on the outer wrappings. Eventually, bodies were preserved with chemicals. It is this later method that is called mummification.

Immediately after death, a body was taken to the funeral workshops on the west side of the Nile. Because the sun set in the west, all bodies were buried there. After each body was washed, the organs—hearts, brains, livers, and so on—were removed and put into a separate coffin within the tomb.

To mummify bodies, priests would cover them with *natron*, which is a combination of sodium and carbon. After soaking in this mixture for forty days, the bodies would be dried out. The body was then washed and packed with resin-coated bandages and sweet-smelling spices. The the outer body was bandaged and covered with jewels. A painted mask was placed over the body's face and it was wrapped once more.

Other priests prepared coffins for the body to rest in. In many cases there were three separate coffins, the first fitting inside the next. Finally, all three would be placed in a large outer coffin.

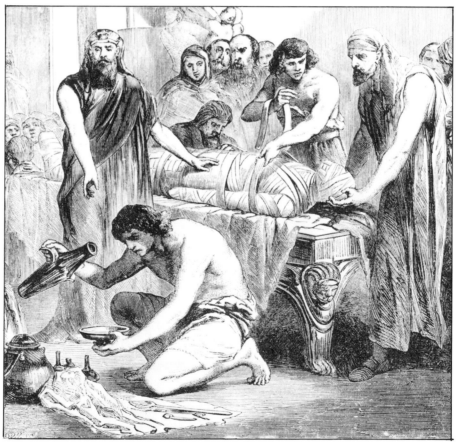

This nineteenth-century engraving shows Egyptian priests wrapping a mummified body in bandages.

use. When archaeologists discovered the remains of an unfinished step pyramid begun shortly after Zoser's reign, they found ramps made of rubble still in place.

Before the first stone of a pyramid could be laid, a site for the tomb had to be chosen. A pyramid site had to meet a number of specific requirements. For religious reasons, a pharaoh's tomb could only be located on the western side of Nile, toward the setting sun. The pharaoh's body was transported to the tomb by boat, so the pyramid had to be close enough to the Nile for a causeway (road) to be built from the river to the pyramid. But the site had to stand higher than the highest flood waters, and the site could not be so high that it would be impossible for workers to move building stones to within a close distance. The site also needed to be level and wide enough to accommodate the smaller tombs of the pharaoh's court. Finally, the ground had to have a solid foundation of rock to support the enormous weight of the pyramid.

For all these reasons, the builders of the tomb of Snefru's son Cheops found that the Giza plateau was the perfect spot for a pyramid for the king. According to Herodotus, the ancient Greek historian, Cheops' pyramid took twenty years to build. It took another ten years to build the causeway which connected the pyramid to a temple in the nearby valley.

While plans for the pyramid were being drawn up, thousands of workers—including stonecutters, surveyors, carpenters, masons, and mortar makers—were sent by towns and villages throughout the land to take part in the construction. In addition to the workers who lived at the pyramid site, between fifty thousand and a hundred thousand workers arrived every year between July and November, when the Nile flooded and farming was impossible. These workers were organized into crews to move stones from a nearby rock quarry to the building site. For their work, the men were paid with food and clothing.

The workmen who built the pyramids used many different tools. Tools for cutting stone were made either of copper or a very hard rock called dolorite. Scribes working for the chief architect wrote instructions for the workers, telling them exactly which kind of stones were needed and how big each block of stone had to be. Most of the stone used in Cheops' pyramid came from nearby quarries, although the finer stone used for the pyramid's outer casing was brought across the Nile from quarries at Moqattam and Tura.

To get the best possible limestone, workers dug tunnels into the sides of cliffs, from which huge blocks were cut, one piece at a time. Gangs of workers used wooden levers and ropes to move each block of stone onto a sled. The sled was then dragged across a row of logs to a boat. (The logs were used so that the sled would not sink into the sand from the great weight.) The boat would then carry the stone across the river to Giza.

The exact position of a pharaoh's pyramid was very important to the Egyp-

This photograph, taken in one the first scientific surveys of the pyramids in the twentieth century, shows the leveled base of the valley floor at Giza.

tians. Any time a pyramid was built, the location of true north had to be found, since the Egyptians believed that the entrance to the pharaoh's tomb should always face the north star. For this reason, the pyramid builders needed not only strong architectural and organizational skills but also an understanding of mathematics and astronomy. A circular wall was built in the center of the site, just high enough to block the view of surrounding hills and create a perfect horizon line. A priest then stood in the center of the circle and waited for the appearance of a star rising in the east. As the star appeared, a line was drawn between where it rose and the center of the circle. The priest would watch the star as it seemed to sink under the opposite wall and then draw a second line from that point to the center of the circle. Because the priests were aware

that stars appear to rotate around the North Pole, they also knew that a third line from the center of the circle and through the space between the first two lines would point directly north.

After determining the direction of true north, the next step was to measure out and level the base of the pyramid. The base of Cheops' Great Pyramid covered a total area of thirteen acres—about the size of ninety football fields.

To make sure the pyramid's base was level, trenches were dug and filled with water. By using the water levels as guides, the architects were able to build the site so evenly that modern experts using sophisticated equipment were able to determine that the southeast corner of the Great Pyramid is just a half inch higher than the northwest corner.

The pyramid builders also had to make sure the site for the pharaoh's mortuary temple was clear as well. Foundations were also built for the valley temple and the causeway. While the pyramid was being built, the base of the valley temple was probably used to unload stones from across the river, and the causeway may have acted as a giant ramp along which the stones could be dragged. Once the stones reached the end of the causeway, they may have been pushed onto wooden rockers from which they could be moved into place more easily. Each stone may then have been rolled from the rocker onto logs which stood over the place where the stones would be laid. A thin coat of mortar was probably spread across the stones. Finally, the logs were removed and the stones were pushed into place. Eventually, the entire ground-level base of the pyramid would be set in place in this way.

Putting the pyramid's first level into place was the easy part. To raise each of the next levels, Cheops' builders used ramps made of rubble held together with mud from the Nile. One ramp was built at each corner of the pyramid and grew up along the side of the pyramid. Logs may have been built into the top of the ramp to help move the sleds that carried such heavy stone, much in the same way that the stones had been dragged from the quarry to the banks of the Nile. Some workmen had the job of extending the ramp farther up the side of the pyramid when each new level was finished. Each time a ramp was finished, crews of twenty or more men pulled the stone-bearing sled while others pushed from behind.

As the years passed, and boys whose fathers had worked on the pyramid grew up to work on the same pyramid themselves, the pyramid finally neared completion. Eventually, as each new level was built smaller than the one below it, two of the ramps were abandoned, because there was no longer room for all four. Finally, after about twenty years, the top stone, or capstone, of the pyramid was ready to be lifted into place. This was a cause for celebration. Prayers were said to honor the event. At last, workers dragged the capstone up to the top of the pyramid. A small piece of stone that stuck out from the bottom of the capstone was fitted into a hole cut on the top level of the pyramid, so that the capstone was to be directly over the center. The Great Pyramid was finished. As they removed the ramps from the side of the pyramid, starting from the top and working downward toward the ground, the workers ground the capstone into a shining peak. Below, others chiseled away the steps of the outer casing of the pyramid, leaving four smooth outer walls.

In fact, the outside of the Great Pyramid closely resembles the second Snefru pyramid built at Dashur. But archaeologists believe not only that the interior of the pyramid differs from previous tombs built for Snefru and Zoser, but also that the builders changed their plans at least two times during construction.

The changes involved the pyramid's most important feature—the pharaoh's burial chamber deep inside the pyra-

An artist's conception of how the pyramids at Giza might have been built.

mid. The first plan called for the chamber to be dug into the ground-level rock on which the pyramid sat. A tunnel was dug from the entrance, slanting downward and finally reaching a small chamber at its end, just as the plan called for. The second plan called for the chamber to be built into the exact center of the pyramid, though not far from ground level. Since a tunnel had already been built from the entrance, there was no way a new tunnel could be dug straight from the entrance to the king's chamber. Instead, a new corridor cut through the ceiling of the descending tunnel, rising up to another horizontal tunnel that in turn led to what has been misnamed the Queen's Chamber. Finally, the last and most ambitious plan involved wooden scaffolding that could be lowered immediately after the pharaoh's funeral to block the ascending staircase, leaving the pharaoh protected for eternity.

Sharing the plateau of Giza with Cheops' Great Pyramid are two others, each built by a succeeding Fourth Dynasty pharaoh. The second oldest was built by Chephren, or Khafre, Cheops' son. Although Chephren's pyramid looks taller than his father's, it is not; it is built on slightly higher ground, and its sides are also built at steeper angles. A special feature of Chephren's pyramid is that it still has some of the original smooth outer casing near its top.

The valley temple of Chephren's funeral complex is a simple building, almost without decoration. Its walls are made of polished granite. A pit in one room contained a set of sculptures of the pharaoh, including one of the most famous Egyptian statues, which shows the king seated with Horus, the falcon god, perched on the back of his throne.

The third and smallest pyramid at Giza was built for the pharaoh Mycerinus, or Menkaure. Even though it appears to have been finished quickly using mud bricks, its valley temple contained a series of beautiful statues. One shows Mycerinus standing between Hathor, a local Memphis goddess, and another woman, who represents one of the provinces of Egypt.

Mycerinus' pyramid itself was refurnished, probably over a thousand years after it was built, during the Twenty-sixth Dynasty. Unfortunately, a sarcophagus, or stone coffin, was lost at sea while being shipped to England centuries later, so the exact date of its construction might never be known. A wooden coffin, originally thought to have belonged to Mycerinus, is now known to have been placed in the tomb about eighteen hundred years after he died. An inscription found in 1968 near the entrance to the tomb refers to this ancient restoration effort.

Guarding the causeway from Pharaoh Chephren's monument is one of the most mysterious monuments the world has ever known. The strange half-man, half-beast limestone figure has been known as the Sphinx ever since it was named by Greek explorers.

According to one theory about the Sphinx's origins, workers on Cheops' pyramid may have begun carving a huge chunk of limestone into the shape of a lion, but the project was apparently abandoned. When Chephren's pyramid was being built, this unfinished sculpture blocked the area in which the causeway and temple were to be built. Unless a use for it could be found, the rock would have to be removed. At this point, Chephren's chief architect may have decided that it would be easier to have the workers finish the sculpture. To the lion's body, they added a human face. Many historians believe the face is that of Chephren.

To the ancient Egyptians, a lion was no ordinary animal. Lions were dangerous and mighty animals that needed no protection from man. In fact, fifteen hundred years after Chephren's death, lions were the favorite prey of pharaohs during royal hunts. That the body of a lion would be combined with the head and face of a man was a uniquely Egyptian idea. It was also an old Egyptian idea. Even before the First Dynasty, rulers were represented by lions.

Lions symbolized not only strength but also protection. They were seen as

The Great Sphinx at Giza with Cheops' pyramid in the background.

supreme guardians. Often, the feet of chairs were sculpted to appear like those of lions, and beds were carved to look like lions' bodies.

The lion was not simply a model for household furniture. Tame lions always went with the pharaoh into battle, granting the king the protection of a god. Many gods were connected with lions. Sekhmet, a goddess of war who was said to bring destruction to all enemies of the almighty sun god Re, was portrayed as having a woman's body and the head of a lion. Lions were also linked with Tefnut, the lion-headed goddess of rain and dew.

A great number of workers carved the great lionlike rock into an image of their pharaoh. When finished, the entire creature, with outstretched paws, measured 240 feet long and over 60 feet high. The creature's head, with a nose about the height of an Egyptian man and lips that stretched seven feet across, showed the features of Chephren, the god-king. Originally, the Sphinx wore a pleated headdress, with a cobra on its top and the traditional false beard that all pharaohs wore.

Although the Sphinx is a man-made monument carved out of rock, it was a "living image" to the ancient Egyptians. In fact, the term "living image" may have been written as "seshepankh," which the Greeks translated as "sphinx." The first written mention of the Sphinx came long after its construction. By then, the link with Chephren had largely been forgotten. The Sphinx's name had become Hor-am-Akhet, or Horus-in-the-Horizon. From that, the Greeks came up with Harmachis, which is what they called their god of the Sphinx.

Egyptians thought it important that the Sphinx was connected to the horizon. The western horizon was the land of the dead, ruled by Osiris, the god of the underworld. In addition, the word for "horizon" in ancient hieroglyphic writing showed a picture of the sun between two hills. The round face of the Sphinx happens to lie right between two hills.

No one knows for sure whether the Egyptians believed that the Sphinx itself was a god. The remains of a Sphinx temple have been found, proving that priests did pay tribute to the figure almost immediately after it was built. In fact, the Sphinx Temple is the oldest nonfuneral temple ever found in Egypt. Built in the Fourth Dynasty, when the unification of Upper and Lower Egypt was still relatively new, the temple has two separate entrances, two outer passages, and two sets of inside chambers. Egypt itself was still seen as two nations joined as one, and the architect of the Sphinx Temple emphasized that in his work.

Many more sphinxes were built by later Egyptians. The Twelfth Dynasty pharaoh Amenemhet III appears to have had his image carved into a great number of sphinxes, and the New Kingdom's female pharaoh, Hatshepsut, may also have modeled for sphinxes. Not all later sphinxes had human heads. At the great New Kingdom temple at Luxor, Ramses the Great built a long avenue of ram-headed creatures.

But no Sphinx has captured people's imagination like the Sphinx at Giza. An ancient legend about the Sphinx gives an idea just how old the structure is. According to the legend, a young prince riding in the desert stopped to nap in the Sphinx's shade. As he slept, the Sphinx spoke to him, promising that if the prince removed the sand that had piled around him, the Sphinx would make him pharaoh. The prince cleared the sand, and soon became Pharaoh Thutmose IV, who ruled Egypt 3,400 years ago. By then, the Sphinx was already over a thousand years old.

As the Fourth Dynasty ended and the Fifth Dynasty began, Egyptian society underwent great changes. The government became more complicated and the growing number of government officials became more wealthy and powerful. In time, these new noblemen began to build great tombs not for their kings but for themselves. By the end of the Sixth Dynasty, which lasted from about 2345 B.C. to 2181 B.C., the growing power of local government officials began to threaten the power of the pharaoh himself. Following the ninety-year reign of Pepi I, central government all but disappeared. The irrigation system necessary to harness the Nile broke down, crops failed, and famine reached Upper Egypt. Civil war soon broke out across the land.

This troubled time, which lasted two hundred years, is known to historians as the First Intermediate Period. During this time, two families attempted to rule from Memphis, but their authority was hardly recognized by the rest of Egypt. Eventually, two more families (the Ninth

A head-on view of the Sphinx. According to some accounts, the monument lost its nose when French soldiers used it for target practice during Napoléon Bonaparte's invasion of Egypt in 1798.

and Tenth Dynasties) established themselves in the town of Herakleopolis, about 55 miles south of Memphis.

Although Egypt would experience other periods of greatness later in its history, none would equal the greatness of the Old Kingdom. For thousands of years to come, even the mightiest of pharaohs would try in vain to recapture the glory of the past. The land of Egypt, united under one pharaoh throughout the Old Kingdom, had lost its way.

CHAPTER THREE

The Triumph of Thebes

The history of ancient Egypt after the end of the Old Kingdom is the story of a land struggling to live up to its dynamic past. The most important characteristic about Old Kingdom Egypt was its orderly, united society. With the coming of the First Intermediate Period about 2181 B.C., the Egyptian people witnessed an almost complete breakdown of their society. The building of the pyramids at Giza only a few short centuries before had shown how the entire nation could work together, according to highly organized and precise laws, when building the resting places of its pharaohs.

Unfortunately, the building of the pyramids placed great strain on the nation's economy. At the same time, local administrators who had ruled in the name of the pharaoh during the Old Kingdom began to rule local nomes as their own private kingdoms. The political organization that had allowed Egypt

This relief from the white temple at Karnak depicts Pharaoh Sesostris I making an offering to the gods.

to harness the Nile, and that had been the signature of the Old Kingdom's glory, was in shambles.

Another change had taken place that struck deeper into the heart of Egyptian society. Even as early as the Fifth Dynasty, the pharaoh was seen as the earthly son of the sun god, Re. If he was Re's son, then he could not be the god's equal at the same time. As Re's importance rose, the pharaoh's spiritual power shrank, because he was no longer seen as the equal of every other god. Meanwhile, the priests that served Re grew in power.

By 2000 B.C., the Egyptian people had suffered two centuries of chaos and civil war. Egypt once again had two warring centers of power. The pharaohs ruling from the Old Kingdom capital of Memphis were as powerless nationwide as the pharaohs that controlled Upper Egypt from Herakleopolis. Local officials governed lands that during the Old Kingdom had been under the solitary rule of one pharaoh. In fact, the pharaohs of this era were so powerless that local administrators even stopped paying taxes to them.

In the Upper Egypt town of Thebes, a new family of pharaohs came to power by defeating the pharaohs ruling from Herakleopolis. The first king of this Eleventh Dynasty was Nebhapetre Mentuhotep. By 2040 B. C., Mentuhotep had reunited Upper and Lower Egypt and re-established a central government. He also began sending trading and mining expeditions to neighboring lands. Ships sent to Byblos, in what is now Lebanon, returned with cedar wood; expeditions to Sinai obtained turquoise and copper; and journeys to nearby Kush and Wawat yielded gold, ebony, animal skins, monkeys, and slaves. Mentuhotep started to rebuild irrigation canals and dikes to ensure abundant crops.

Although later pharaohs would build pyramids, Mentuhotep's funeral complex did not include a pyramid. Still, it is considered his greatest achievement. His funeral site at Deir al-Bahri, across the Nile from Thebes, features a causeway leading to the main complex of buildings. Mentuhotep's tomb consisted of three terraces with columns. All around the courtyard stood statues of the king, and beautiful reliefs (statues chiseled from a wall) graced the insides of the buildings. The period known as the Middle Kingdom (2133–1786 B.C.) had begun.

Although Thebes remained the spiritual center of Egypt, the kings of the Twelfth Dynasty—which was begun by Amenemhet I in 1991 B. C.—moved their capital north to Lisht, which is about twenty miles from Memphis. In fact, the builders of Amenemhet's pyramid used many of the old decorated blocks from earlier royal tombs from Memphis in constructing his pyramid. Because Memphis was so close, Amenemhet found that these older sites provided a source of cheap, convenient building material.

During his reign, Amenemhet I proved to be one of the Middle Kingdom's most important pharaohs. He and his successors reorganized the nation's laws to reduce the power of local administrators and nobles and give more authority to local officials, village leaders, and town councils.

Over the centuries, Thebes's role as the spiritual center of Egypt made it the most important of the nation's cities. The pharaohs of the Twelfth Dynasty believed that Amon, the god of Thebes, had been responsible for reuniting the nation. As the influence of Thebes grew, Amon became a national god. Eventually, the identities of Amon and Re, the Old Kingdom god of the sun, would merge into one and become known as Amon-Re. The Temple of Amon-Re, which began modestly about 2000 B.C. north of Thebes in the village of Karnak, grew into an immense complex containing the richest temple in all Egypt.

Although few monuments dating from the Middle Kingdom remain standing today—Mentuhotep's Deir el Bahri complex is in complete ruin—the Pharaoh Sesostris I's white temple has been restored. The blocks that make up

This road was built to give access to the tombs at Deir al-Bahri near Thebes. By placing tombs in such rugged areas, pharaohs of the later dynasties hoped to avoid grave robbers.

the temple were found among the foundation stones of another Karnak monument. Its walls are decorated with reliefs that depict the king offering tribute to Amon.

By building great structures, unifying Egypt, and expanding trade, the rulers of the Twelfth Dynasty helped to restore the nation to some of its former greatness. Unfortunately, the Twelfth Dynasty's achievements didn't last. With the coming of the Thirteenth Dynasty, the nation slipped into another period of weak leaders. Once again the nation became politically divided, with one family of pharaohs at Thebes controlling a strip of territory just 125 miles long. In the north, a rival dynasty took power.

For the first time, it was a dynasty of foreigners. Called the Hyksos, which means chiefs of foreign lands, these rulers were probably from Palestine. They eventually won control of much of the Nile delta. The Hyksos' well-trained army introduced new weapons to Egypt, including body armor, powerful bows made of horn and wood, and horse-drawn war chariots.

Only three pyramids are known to have been built during the Thirteenth Dynasty. The pyramid of Pharaoh Amenyqemau is at Dashur, although it appears to have never been finished. The other two are at Saqqara, one of which was built for the Pharaoh Khedjer. The other one is badly damaged, and its

41

The restored white chapel at Karnak, built by Pharaoh Sesostris I.

builder is unknown. These three pyramids were the last ones ever built in Egypt.

Even with their advantage in weaponry, the Hyksos were never able to control all of Egypt or defeat the monarchs at Thebes. In about 1590 B.C., the Pharoah Ahmose I came out of Thebes to battle the Hyksos. Wielding the Hyksos weapons, which they had learned to use, Ahmosis' army drove the Hyksos out of Egypt. With this victory, Egypt was freed from 150 years of foreign rule. From then on, Thebes replaced Memphis as the political and religious capital of Egypt. The nation was once again united. As the first ruler of the Eighteenth Dynasty, Ahmose ushered in one of the greatest and most turbulent periods of Egyptian history—the New Kingdom.

During the Old Kingdom, there had been little reason for Egypt to have a large army. The country had been protected from invasion by the desert and the sea. And the Egyptians never needed to invade other lands, because the rich banks of the Nile produced all the food they needed. While soldiers did join in expeditions to Nubia for gold, or to the Sinai for copper or turquoise, Egypt was for the most part a peaceful nation. In fact, this peaceful atmosphere was one of the most important reasons that the Old Kingdom Egyptians were able to build the great

A later drawing of one of the string of fortresses that guarded Egypt's southern border during the New Kingdom.

pyramids: They could focus the nation's wealth and manpower on construction, not on war.

When the rulers of Thebes chased the Hyksos out of Egypt, all that changed. During the Middle Kingdom, Egypt built a line of fortresses to protect its southern border with Nubia. These forts housed not only soldiers but also government officials and scribes. In time, these garrisons became powerful and influential.

The Egyptian attitude toward war had changed. The Egypt of the New Kingdom was much more aggressive. Troops were sent to conquer Syria and Palestine and to dominate Nubia. For the first time, a large, permanent army was organized.

During the New Kingdom, one of the chief roles of the pharaoh was as commander of the army. The Old Kingdom pharaoh had been an all-powerful ruler. Even though he made the laws of the land and all Egypt actually belonged to him, he was also a god, somewhat distant from the everyday lives of his people. Day-to-day administration of the nation was handled largely by his vizier and local governors.

The New Kingdom pharaoh was still the owner of all lands in the kingdom. But at the same time, he now personally led the nation into battle in foreign

This tomb relief from Karnak shows Queen Hatshepsut wearing the traditional false beard of the pharaoh.

lands. In fact, waging war became practically the first priority for almost all pharaohs from the New Kingdom on. After defeating the Hyksos, Pharaoh Ahmose recaptured all the lands that Egypt had lost since the Old Kingdom. His successors, Amenhotep I and Thutmose I, were also great warriors. They pushed the country's borders even farther south and northeast to Palestine and Syria. With those reigns, Egypt began a period of good fortune that would last for 150 years.

One of Egypt's next pharaohs was quite different from all previous Egyptian rulers. In fact, Pharaoh Hatshepsut was not a king at all. She was a Queen, the daughter of Thutmose I.

The only woman to rule Egypt—before the famous Cleopatra many years later—Hatshepsut was married to Thutmose II, a weak and unimportant pharaoh. When he died, his son, Thutmose III, was only a small child, too young to rule on his own. Hatshepsut became the regent (caretaker) of the government. Two years later, she took the throne officially for herself and claimed the title of pharaoh.

Some historians think that many Egyptians were uncomfortable with a female pharaoh. This may be because

A panoramic view of the temple complex built near Thebes by Hatshepsut.

during the earliest days of Egypt's founding, the male pharaoh was believed to bring strong, growing crops and animal herds to his people. It seems that the queen realized this, because she was usually portrayed in statues as a male. Some statues even show her wearing the pharaoh's traditional false beard.

During her reign, Hatshepsut withdrew many of Egypt's armies from battles in foreign lands. She also worked to keep open the trade routes that had been closed during the years the Hyksos ruled Egypt and built impressive monuments and other public works.

Like the Eleventh Dynasty pharaoh Nebhapetre Mentuhotep, Hatshepsut built a temple at Deir al-Bahri. Hers is one of Egypt's most beautiful buildings. Partly cut into the surrounding rock cliffs, the mortuary is a unique blend of human construction and natural surroundings. Because of its enormous size, Hatshepsut's temple has been compared to the Old Kingdom pyramids of Giza. Of course, Hatshepsut built her tomb for the same reason that Old Kingdom pharaohs like Zoser, Snefru, and Cheops had built their pryamids—as an eternal home for her ka, or spirit.

There are a number of reasons that Queen Hatshepsut and other New Kingdom pharaohs stopped building pyramids as their final resting places. In many ways, the pyramids had proved to be an expensive failure. The rows of pyramids along the west bank of the Nile in Lower Egypt were well-known sources of treasure for tomb robbers—people who made up in greed what they lacked in religious belief. When the capital moved south to Thebes after the Hyksos invaded and occupied the north, another problem had to be solved. In the north, where the banks of the Nile were wide and green, there was much more room to build pyramids. But in the south, across the river from the temples of Thebes, the banks were narrow and surrounded by rugged cliffs. On the other side of a 1,300-foot-high mountain lay an easily guarded valley. The valley became the richest site of buried treasure the world has ever known.

Instead of showcasing their burial sites like the Old Kingdom pharaohs did by building their pyramids, New Kingdom rulers hid them. Tombs were concealed at the ends of long underground tunnels. Decorated inside with mirrors that brought sunlight deep underground, the New Kingdom tombs did not have entrance temples like the pyramids did. After burials, tomb entrances were covered over and made to look like the rocky floor of the desert valley.

During her reign, Hatshepsut had many powerful supporters. One of them, her top aide, was a man named Senemut. By some accounts, Senemut was such a favorite of the queen that he had over eighty official titles. In his job as Minister of Public Works, he assisted Hatshepsut in building the temple at Deir al-Bahri. But during the tomb's construction, Senemut sneaked carvings of himself onto the walls. When the queen heard of this, she not only had as many carvings as could be found removed from her temple but also ordered workers to wreck Senemut's tomb.

Queen Hatshepsut's interest in commerce and construction marked a return to the ways of the Old Kingdom, when Egypt had been able to ignore the outside world except for peaceful trade. The pharaohs of the Twelfth Dynasty and the Middle Kingdom, who kept Upper and Lower Egypt united after many years of rivalry and chaos, also tried to concentrate the land's energies within its borders.

Queen Hatshepsut kept Thutmose III from the throne for twenty years. Finally, he gained enough support to claim his throne. Because inscriptions of the walls of Egyptian temples rarely record negative news, no one knows exactly what happened to Hatshepsut. She may have died of old age, or she may have been murdered. All that is known is that after Thutmose III came to power, he had every mention of Hatshepsut that he could find erased from monument walls.

Thutmose III became one of the greatest military leaders in Egypt's history. His reign marked a return to foreign adventures and conquest. At his death, Egypt's empire stretched from Nubia in the south to just north of the Euphrates River in Syria.

Thutmose celebrated his victories by greatly expanding the Temple of Amon-Re at Karnak. The pharaohs of the Middle Kingdom believed Amon had reunited Upper and Lower Egypt; Thutmose believed that Amon-Re, as he became known after being linked to the Old Kingdom god Re, was responsible for his military strength. Thutmose's greatest building accomplishment was the Hypostyle Hall, which featured 134 columns, some so huge that one hundred men could stand on the top of them, sixty-nine feet above the ground.

In many ways, the pharaohs of the New Kingdom hoped to revive the glory of the Old Kingdom through military means. At the same time, these wars changed the face of Egyptian society in a way that prevented it forever from returning to the ways of the Old Kingdom. As the lands of Egypt stretched to the northeast into Asia and to the south toward the heart of Africa, the risk of invasion by foreign enemies grew. And when kings like Thutmose III looked abroad for foreign lands to conquer, they put pressure on the country's system of government. With more land

A bust of Thutmose III, Hatshepsut's son and one of the most dynamic pharaohs of the New Kingdom.

under Egyptian rule, more local civil servants were needed to enforce Egyptian law.

Such was Thutmose's skill as a ruler that the pharaohs who followed him were able to keep all of these forces in check for a full century after his death. His great-grandson, Amenhotep III, who ruled in the fourteenth century B.C., reigned in peace, dedicating himself almost entirely to building—from his funeral temple to magnificent statues and temples in other cities throughout Egypt.

The new territories also brought Egypt enormous wealth. For each new

A drawing from a tomb painting shows an Egyptian ship being loaded with a cargo that includes wild animals.

triumph, however, the gods were given their tributes. Thutmose III and his successors had good reason to feel that they had restored Ma'at, the order of the universe that had been lost after the end of the Old Kingdom. It was the job of the priests to protect the ma'at once it was regained. New temples were built throughout the empire, and each was filled with splendid treasures.

As soon as the New Kingdom pharaohs looked beyond Egypt for new conquests, the nation couldn't help but change. Even the pharaoh himself began to be seen differently. The pyramid builders of the Old Kingdom had been thought of as gods on Earth. By the time of the New Kingdom, the pharaoh was still thought to be divine, but he was also recognized as a human being capable of making mistakes.

One of the biggest strengths of the Old Kingdom had been the enormous confidence of its people. They had tamed the Nile, built the pyramids, and

even figured out a way for the spirits of their kings to live forever. Unlike New Kingdom Egypt, they had little cause to worry about outsiders.

During the New Kingdom, contact with foreigners was a fact of life. Chariots traveled back and forth between Egypt, its foreign territories, and its neighbors. Ships sailed up and down the Nile, bringing goods from outside Egypt's borders. As long as Egypt had a strong king like Thutmose, no outside enemy dared to challenge it.

When Amenhotep III's son, Amenhotep IV, came to power, Egypt's grip on its empire began to slip. Powerful enemies, like the Hittites in Asia Minor, took hold of Syria. It soon became clear that Amenhotep IV was more concerned with another issue besides defending Egyptian territory.

Some historians believe that Amenhotep IV may have been mentally unstable. Others see him as a great genius whose thinking was ahead of his time.

Amenhotep IV was deeply religious. Unlike previous pharaohs, however, he did not believe in the system of many gods that had been practiced for centuries. Most of all, he did not believe in Amon-Re. The new pharaoh even had Amon-Re's name erased from most monuments throughout the land.

Amenhotep IV believed that there was only one god, named Aton, who was the god of the sun and the source of all life. So strongly did he believe this that he changed his name from Amenhotep, meaning "Amon is content, the god ruler of Thebes," to Akhenaton, which means "Serviceable to Aton." He also moved the capital away from Thebes to a new city, which he called Akhetaton, or "the Horizon of Aton." Akhetaton is near the present-day site of Tell el-Amarna.

Akhenaton felt that the pharaohs had lost too much of their religious power to priests that served gods like Amon-Re. He was determined to restore the pharaoh's religious role to what it had been during the Old Kingdom. Most priests and civil servants were strongly opposed to the vast changes in religious worship that he hoped to put into place. These priests had become especially strong since the days of Thutmose III.

What made Akhenaton's job even more difficult was that he refused to allow the common people to worship Aton directly. Instead, they were asked to worship Akhenaton alone, because he considered himself the earthly representative of the god, just as Old Kingdom pharaohs were representatives of Re.

This relief of the pharaoh Akhenaton and his queen, Nefertiti, shows the more natural artistic style that developed during his reign.

There were great changes during Akhenaton's reign. These changes were apparent not only in religious worship. The art of the period was also vastly different. Before Akhenaton, portrayals of the pharaohs were usually idealized portraits—pictures that showed not what the person looked like but how the holy figure should appear to his followers. During the reign of Akhenaton, which is known to history as the Amarna period, sculptures and paintings of the pharaoh and other Egyptians are more realistic.

Even though he was pictured in many traditional poses—such as a hunter, a warrior, or a sphinx—many of the portraits of Akhenaton show him with his beautiful wife, Nefertiti, and their family. Since he believed that as a living god all his actions were important, pictures

This page from The Book of the Dead *shows the dead being judged by the god Osiris.*

of him hugging his children, or driving in a chariot with Nefertiti, were just as acceptable as subjects.

Akhenaton was only in power for sixteen years. When he died, his religious revolution died with him. For all of his personal religious belief, he had never been able to inspire ordinary Egyptians to abandon their old gods. Akhenaton's belief in the Aton gave little to the common people to believe themselves. Artwork showing the Aton showed it blessing only the pharaoh and his family, not ordinary Egyptians. Also, not only did Akhenaton openly attack Amon-Re, but he completely ignored the one god that the common people had loved most dearly throughout the ages—Osiris, the protector of the dead. There is no mention of Osiris in Akhenaton's tomb or in the tombs of any of his nobles. In fact, all those tombs were deliberately built

on the east side of the Nile, not on the western side traditionally associated with Osiris.

Osiris' continuing importance during the New Kingdom is clear from the New Kingdom's use of texts that had been written on temple walls during the Old Kingdom. These texts gave powerful spells to the thousands who could afford to be buried with them.

The most famous of these texts is *The Book of the Dead.* A collection of spells, formulas, and prayers, it was intended to help the departed leave their tombs by day to renew life. The book shows that the Egyptians of the New Kingdom were just as attached to the idea of life after death as their Old Kingdom predecessors.

There was one major difference, however. While only the pharaoh was reborn as Osiris during the Old Kingdom, by the New Kingdom, all Egyptians were granted the promise of eternal life. Like the pharaohs of old, the mortal who took *The Book of the Dead* to the grave became one with the sun.

Akhenaton's religious revolution failed because the belief that each ordinary citizen would live eternally in the Land of the Dead was just too important to be given up, especially by a people who were already worried about the threats from invaders at their borders. Upon Akenhaton's death, the young pharaoh Tutankhamen moved the capital back to Thebes and reintroduced the worship of Amon and the traditional gods. Little else is known of Tutankhamen. He died young after ruling with little achievement.

Today, this boy king may be the best-known pharaoh of all. In 1922, English archaeologist Howard Carter discovered his tomb in the Valley of the Kings. No other pharaoh's tomb has been found in such a near-intact state. In it, Carter found the burial chamber—a huge shrine, covered in gold. In other rooms, he found beds, chariots, ebony and ivory stools, vases, and other important artifacts.

Because Tutankhamen left no heirs to his throne, the Eighteenth Dynasty passed into history shortly after his reign. The Nineteenth Dynasty saw Egypt's last great period of empire. Ramses II was both one of the strongest pharaohs in Egyptian history and also the last native Egyptian king to rule with such power.

Ramses II, or Ramses the Great, was an active warrior. He tried to win back

The golden mask of Tutankhamen.

control of southern Syria, which had been lost during Akhenaton's reign. He also campaigned against the city of Kadesh, which was in territory controlled by the Hittite empire. The battle appears to have been a draw. Ramses saw the battle's outcome differently. To honor his self-declared victory, Ramses carved an enormous temple in the cliffs at Abu Simbel. In the front of the temple he built four seated statues of himself.

The last major ruler of The New Kingdom was Ramses III. This Ramses was forced to defend Egypt against invaders known as the Sea People. Ramses's army and navy were able to push back the invaders out of the Nile Delta. But by the war's end, Egypt was again a changed country. No longer would it look overseas for foreign conquests. For the remainder of their history, the ancient Egyptians would either have to defend their soil from invaders, or, as would be true more often than not, be ruled by them.

CHAPTER FOUR

The Decline of an Empire

He had beaten back the invading Sea People. He had given great treasures to the nation's temples. Still, by the end of Ramses III's successful thirty-one year reign, the pharaoh faced many great difficulties. When their monthly food rations became overdue, workers building the royal tombs went on strike. The strike only ended when the vizier personally stepped in. More important, a plot to kill the pharaoh was discovered.

Although Pharaoh Ramses III followed Ramses the Great by only a few short years, and although his long reign was a successful one, he would be the last pharaoh to rule over a powerful, united Egypt.

During this period Egypt became more and more unstable. By the reign of the last Ramses, power in Lower Egypt was held by the vizier of Lower Egypt, while the High Priest of Amun, who ruled from Thebes, controlled Upper Egypt. So powerless was the pharaoh himself that he almost completely withdrew to his royal palace in the Nile Delta.

These huge columns are part of the complex built by Ramses II at Abu Simbel to mark his military victories.

The central government became so weak that rival kings ruled different cities. Before long, people from Libya, a land west of Egypt, began to settle in the Nile Delta. By the year 950 B.C., Libyan families gained control over the region, which they ruled for over two centuries.

The Libyans were only the first group of foreigners to rule Egypt. By the Twenty-fifth Dynasty, the pharaohs of Egypt came from Nubia, which had long been an Egyptian colony. In 663 B.C., however, the Assyrian king Assurbanipal moved his army into Egypt and attacked Memphis and Thebes.

In time, the power of the Assyrians declined, and a new dynasty—the Twenty-sixth—was formed by a family of kings from Saïs in the western Nile Delta. With these kings came the last great period of Egyptian history. The Saite kings were able to reunite Upper and Lower Egypt once again. But another enemy had risen up in the east—the Babylonian Empire. Led by King Nebuchadrezzar, the armies of Babylon invaded and occupied Egypt in 605 B.C.

Babylonian rule lasted less than a century. In 539 B.C., Babylon itself fell to

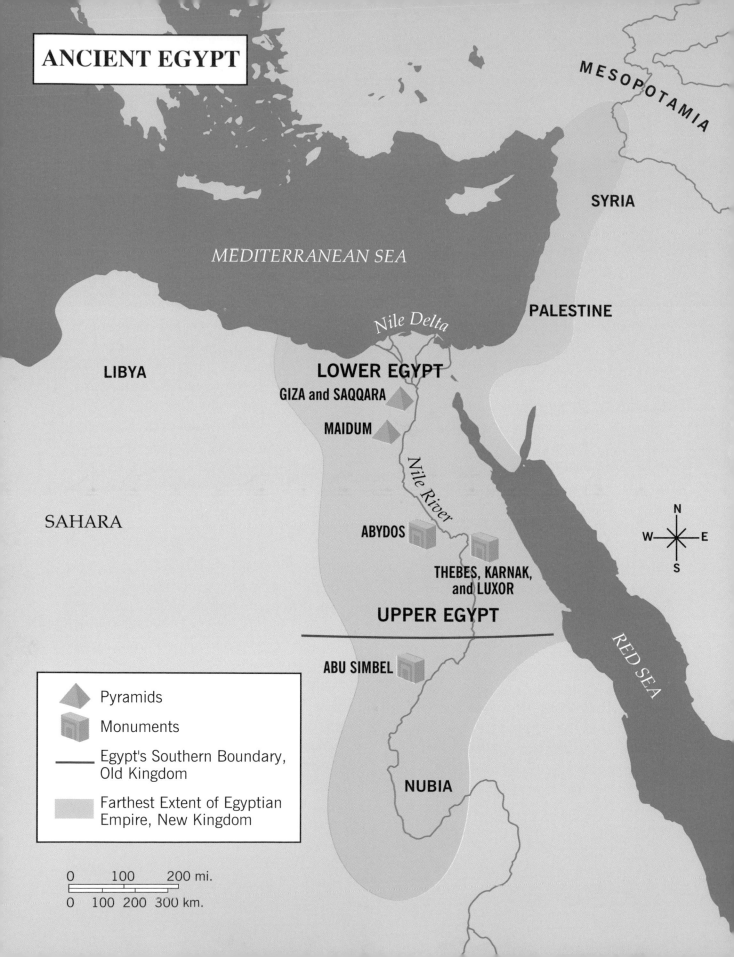

ANCIENT EGYPT

MESOPOTAMIA

SYRIA

PALESTINE

MEDITERRANEAN SEA

LIBYA

Nile Delta

LOWER EGYPT

GIZA and SAQQARA

MAIDUM

Nile River

SAHARA

ABYDOS

THEBES, KARNAK,
and LUXOR

UPPER EGYPT

ABU SIMBEL

RED SEA

NUBIA

N
W · E
S

Pyramids

Monuments

Egypt's Southern Boundary,
Old Kingdom

Farthest Extent of Egyptian
Empire, New Kingdom

| 0 | 100 | 200 mi. |

| 0 | 100 | 200 | 300 km. |

the Persian king Cyrus, and in 525 B.C., his son Cambyses attacked and defeated Egypt.

After its capture, Egypt was ruled by a Persian *satrap* (governor). The Persians regularly collected taxes from Egypt and ran the country mostly according to Egyptian law. After several unsuccessful rebellions, the Egyptians finally drove the Persians out.

Although the Egyptians had driven out invaders yet again, the nation remained weak. The last Egyptian dynasties depended on mercenary Greek soldiers for their defense. Hiring foreigners as soldiers cost the nation dearly, and for a brief time, beginning in 341 B.C., Persia regained control. Just nine years later, Alexander the Great, leader of the Greeks, brought his army into Egypt and defeated the Persians once and for all. Although he was a foreigner, the Egyptians welcomed Alexander as a hero.

Alexander kept together most of the Egyptian system of government, but he kept ultimate power in his own hands. Although he personally did not stay long in Egypt, he began construction of a new city, Alexandria, on the Mediterranean coast. Alexandria became a major commercial city and the intellectual center of the Mediterranean. When Alexander died, he was succeeded by Ptolemy, one of his generals. Ptolemy brought Alexander's body to Egypt to be buried.

For the next 250 years, Egypt was ruled by the descendants of Ptolemy. Unlike previous foreign rulers, the Ptolomaic pharaohs, as they are known, ruled Egypt not simply as a conquered territory of a foreign land but as an independent nation. In fact, the Greeks took care to preserve many of the ancient Egyptian traditions. They also had many of their monument inscriptions carved in Greek as well as in hieroglyphics. One such inscription, dating from the reign of Ptolemy V in 196 B.C., was found on what is today known as Rosetta Stone. By comparing the languages in the Rosetta Stone, the French scholar Jean François de Chompollion was able to discover the clue to the meaning of the ancient writing in 1822.

Under the Ptolemys, the nation's agriculture and commerce thrived. Alexandria became one of the world's great cities. The city's huge library attracted thinkers from many other countries. It was in Alexandria that the Old Testament of the Bible was first translated into Greek. The Ptolemys encouraged building and continued to care for the ancient temples to win support from the priests who tended them.

Meanwhile, a new power, Rome, had risen in the Mediterranean. In 30 B.C., the Roman navy destroyed the navy of Queen Cleopatra VIII. Cleopatra and her Roman husband Marc Antony were killed. Egypt fell into the hands of Octavian, who later became the Roman Emperor Augustus.

Octavian treated Egypt as his own personal kingdom. All wealth from Egyptian trade and agriculture went to Rome, and the people of Egypt grew poorer. Over time, one of the greatest civilizations the world has ever known passed into history.

Rediscovering Ancient Egypt

When Queen Cleopatra died, so did over 3,000 years of continuous rule under the pharaohs. In many ways, the magnificent civilization of Egypt had disappeared much earlier. From the tenth century B.C. until the coming of the Romans, the religious, cultural, and political traditions of ancient Egypt were slowly lost.

Despite the political changes that came to Egypt with each new invasion, the daily life of most Egyptians didn't change much, regardless of whether Persians, Libyans, or Babylonians ran the government. More important were the comings and goings of the floods and the maintenance of the nation's irrigation system.

In the sixth century B.C., for example, the Persians introduced the *saquiah*—a series of wheels, moved by

Two of the statues at the Abu Simbel complex. Abu Simbel became the focus of modern rescue archaeology efforts during the building of the Aswan Dam in the 1960s, which flooded the area.

oxen, that lifted water from one level and emptied it on another. In later years, the *tambour*, or *Archimedes* screw, was introduced. That invention could lift water over short distances. The biggest change for those working the land in Egypt occurred in the twentieth century. In 1968, the Egyptian government built the Aswan Dam. The dam catches water from Lake Nasser, thus allowing the waters of the Nile to be controlled mechanically. Today, because of the Aswan Dam, the annual floods don't occur. The dam has also brought electricity to villages that used to have none. The mud brick houses, built along the river in the same way that they were five thousand years ago, now have television antennas on their roofs.

Development of the Aswan Dam has caused problems as well. Until 1968, the annual floods washed away salt deposits in the soil. Today, however, the soil on the Nile banks is becoming saltier all the time, leading some experts to worry that this once rich soil will one day be desert.

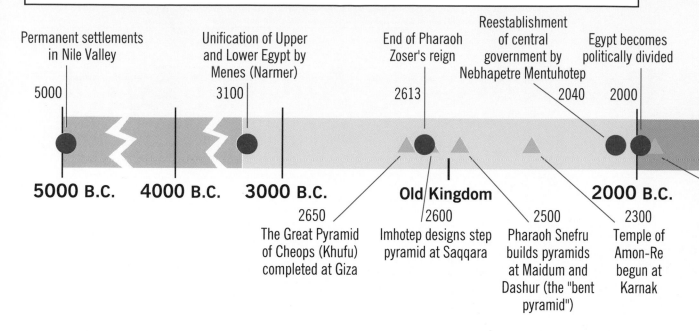

A TIMELINE OF EGYPTIAN HISTORY, 5000 B.C.–30 B.C.

Permanent settlements in Nile Valley
5000

Unification of Upper and Lower Egypt by Menes (Narmer)
3100

End of Pharaoh Zoser's reign
2613

Reestablishment of central government by Nebhapetre Mentuhotep
2040

Egypt becomes politically divided
2000

5000 B.C.   **4000 B.C.**   **3000 B.C.**   **Old Kingdom**   **2000 B.C.**

2650
The Great Pyramid of Cheops (Khufu) completed at Giza

2600
Imhotep designs step pyramid at Saqqara

2500
Pharaoh Snefru builds pyramids at Maidum and Dashur (the "bent pyramid")

2300
Temple of Amon-Re begun at Karnak

A sample of hieroglyphic writing. It was not until 1822, when hieroglyphics were first deciphered by a French scholar, that ancient Egyptian texts could be read.

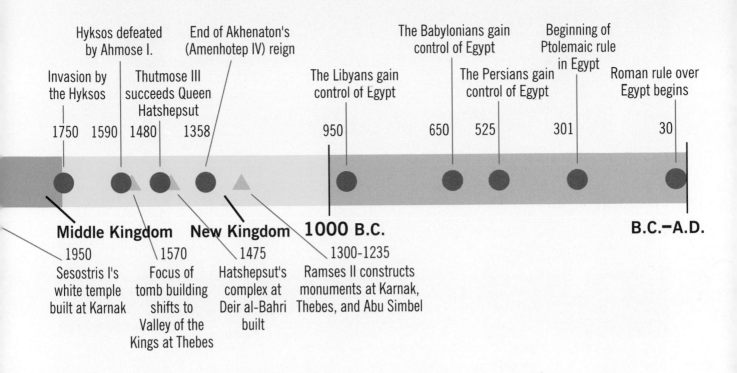

Invasion by the Hyksos — 1750

Hyksos defeated by Ahmose I. — 1590

Thutmose III succeeds Queen Hatshepsut — 1480

End of Akhenaton's (Amenhotep IV) reign — 1358

The Libyans gain control of Egypt — 950

The Babylonians gain control of Egypt — 650

The Persians gain control of Egypt — 525

Beginning of Ptolemaic rule in Egypt — 301

Roman rule over Egypt begins — 30

Middle Kingdom · **New Kingdom** · **1000 B.C.** · **B.C.–A.D.**

1950 — Sesostris I's white temple built at Karnak

1570 — Focus of tomb building shifts to Valley of the Kings at Thebes

1475 — Hatshepsut's complex at Deir al-Bahri built

1300–1235 — Ramses II constructs monuments at Karnak, Thebes, and Abu Simbel

Another big difference between Egypt today and the Egypt of the pharaohs is the Islamic religion. In A.D. 642, the Christian governors representing the Eastern Roman Empire were driven out Egypt by Muslim Arabs. Today, most Egyptians belong to the Islamic faith, and mosques are a main feature of the Egyptian landscape. In fact, there is even a mosque built within the walls of the ancient temple at Luxor.

In the face of the enormous changes brought by history, experts on Egyptian history and culture are racing against time to save the remnants of the ancient past. Through the centuries, many artifacts have been completely lost. Others have never been found. Luckily, because of Egypt's dry climate, many clues to Egypt's past have been preserved. But many of the royal burial tombs have been looted for the enormous riches they contained.

Partly because of this situation, it has been only recently that much has been learned about Egypt's past. With the disappearance of Egyptian traditions, the ancient Egyptian language vanished. Although hieroglyphics remained intact, no one could read them. Many centuries passed before the secrets of Egypt were rediscovered.

By the end of the eighteenth century, interest in Egypt suddenly increased. When Napoleon Bonaparte invaded Egypt in 1798, two hundred scholars accompanied his army. They explored the pyramids and other ruins and described

Modern interest in preserving ancient Egypt's monuments grew in the early decades of the twentieth century. Here, members of the British royal family tour Giza in 1933.

what they had found. Soon ancient Egyptian treasures became popular with Europeans, not so much for what they could teach about the Egyptian civilization but because they were exotic and beautiful. Much of the evidence of Egypt's past was destroyed by overzealous explorers who opened pyramids with battering rams to get at the treasures inside.

Luckily, the looting of tombs was replaced by more scientific methods. The work of Howard Carter, who uncovered the tomb of Tutankhamen, is a good example of patient scientific discovery.

Not every piece of evidence comes from archaeology. For some of their information, historians have had to rely on what the ancient Egyptians themselves wrote. Many of the kings wrote about the great events and victories during their reigns. Ramses the Great is one of the best-known pharaohs mostly because he wrote so much about himself.

As the rate of modern-day construction increases, a new type of archaeology has gained in importance. Rescue archaeology involves teams of historians, archaeologists, and other experts on ancient Egypt working together to help save the ancient monuments. When the Aswan Dam was built in the 1950s and 1960s, for example, a huge lake was formed, endangering many of the treasures of the Nile valley. An international effort was made to protect Egypt's past. One temple was dragged to a site several miles from the banks of the Nile, while others have been dismantled and completely rebuilt elsewhere.

The Temple of Isis at Karnak was one of the monuments affected by the Aswan Dam.

Perhaps the most amazing feat of preservation centered on Ramses the Great's two temples at Abu Simbel. The temples were cut from a cliff into many pieces, some of which weighed as much as 30 tons, and then reconstructed on the top of the cliff.

Today, as historians and archaeologists fight to preserve Egypt's great past, one can not help but think back to the Old Kingdoms pharaohs and architects. Today, the names of Zoser, Imhotep, Cheops, Chephren, and Menkaure live on as they have through the centuries. In many ways, the spirits of the pyramid builders, and the legacy of the extraordinary civilization that they created, endure even now.

INDEX

Page numbers in *Italics* indicate illustrations

Abu Simbel, 51, 53, 57, 61
afterlife, 7, 22, 28, 51
Ahmose I, 42, 44
Akhenaton, 48, *49*, 49-51
Alexander the Great, 55
Alexandria, 55
Amarna period, 49
Amenemhet I, 40
Amenhotep I, 44
Amenhotep III, 47, 48
Amenhotep IV. *See* Akhenaton
Amonhemet III, 36
ancient Egypt, 54
  reunification, 40, 54
  unification, 13, 17, 36, 42
animals revered by the
  Egyptians, 19, 34, 45
Arabs, Muslim, 59
archaeologists, 23, 30, 32, 51, 61
architect, 23-24, 30, 34, 36
army, 43, 45, 47, 55, 60
art, 18, 46, *48*, 49
artifacts, 51, 59
Assurbanipal, 53
Aswan Dam, 57, 60
Augustus, 55

ba, 28
Bonaparte, Napoléon, 37, 60
The Book of the Dead, 50, 51
building materials, 40
  limestone, 22, 30, 34
  mud brick, 12, 23, 34, 57
  stone, 18, 23, 25, 27, 30, 32, 40
burial methods, 28-29

Cairo, 9, 13
Cambyses, 55
capitals of Ancient Egypt, 15, 40,
  46, 51
capstone, 32
Carter, Howard, 51, 60
causeway, 30, 32, 34, 40
ceremonies, 8, 18, 47
chariots, 41, 48
Cheops, 9, 27, 30, 31, 32, 46, 61
Cheops, pyramid of, 6, 7, 30, 33,
  35, 35
Chephren, 9, 34, 35, 61
civil war, 36, 39

class structure, 13, 17-18, 20
Cleopatra, 44, 55, 57
coffins, 7, *28*, 29, 34
columns, 47, *52*
commander-in-chief, 18, 43
commerce, 40, 46, 48, 55
  See also trade
conquests, 43, 47
crops grown, 12
Cyrus, 55

Dashur, 25, 26, 32, 41
death, 28
Deir al-Bahri, 40, *41*, 45, 46
delta. *See* Nile, delta
dynasties, 8, 17, 34
  Eighteenth, 42, 51
  Old Kingdom, 15, 23, 27, 36

education, 18, 20
Egypt, history
  First Intermediate Period, 36,
    39
  Middle Kingdom, 8, 40, 43, 47
  New Kingdom, 8, 36, 43, 48
  Old Kingdom, 8, 9, 15, 17, 21,
    37, 39, 42, 46, 47, 48
Egyptian empire, 42, 43, 47, 53
Egyptian society, 9, 18, 22

false beard, 35, 45
famine, 36
fertility, 13
floods, annual, 11, 12, 13, 30, 57
foreign conquests, 51
fortresses, *43*, 43
funeral complex, 22, 23, 34, 40,
  47

Giza, 9, 27, 30, 33, 34, 35, 36, 46,
  60
gods, 18, 19, 20, 34, 35, 40, 41,
  47, 49, 50
  Amon (Amon-Re), 40, 41, 47, 51
  Aton, 49, 50
  Horus, 19, 26, 34
  major, *19*, 19, 20, 26, 34, 36, 50
  Osiris, *19*, 20, 36, 50
  pharaoh's role as, 13, 43, 48
  Re, 18, 19, 26, 39

government, 17, 36, 39
  local officials, 18, 39, 40, 43, 49
  nomes, 13, 17, 39
  pharaoh, 43
  vizier, 17, 43, 53
grave robbing, 41, 46, 60
Great Pyramid, 9, 32, 33

Hatshepsut, 36, 44-47
Herakleopolis, 37, 39, 40
Herodotus, 8, 9, 13, 30
hieroglyphic writing, 9, 18, 36,
  55, *59*, 59
historians
  ancient, 8, 9, 13, 27, 30
  modern, 24, 25, 34, 60, 61
horizon, 35, 36
Hypostyle Hall, 47

Imhotep, 23-24
invaders of Egypt, 47, 51, 54
  Assyrians, 53
  Babylonians, 54, 57
  French, 37, 60
  Greeks, 35, 55
  Hittites, 48, 51
  Hyksos, 41, 42, 43, 44, 45
  Libyans, 52, 53, 57
  Persians, 55, 57
  Romans, 55, 57
  Sea People, 51, 53
  Syria, 43, 44, 47, 48, 51
irrigation methods, 12-13, 18, 36,
  40, 57, 60
Islam, 59

ka, 21, 22, 28, 46
Kadesh, 51
Karnak, 40, 41, 47
Karnak, white temple of, 39, 40,
  42
Khafre. *See* Chephren
Khufu. *See* Cheops
kings, foreign, 42, 53-55

land of the dead, 22, 28, 36, 51
law, Egyptian, 15, 17, 18, 55
legends, 13, 36
Lower Egypt, 11, 13, 36, 46
Luxor, 36, 59

Ma'at, 17, 48
Maidum, 24, 25
Manetho, 8
Marc Antony, 55
mastabas, 22-23
Memphis, 13, 15, 23, 36, 37, 39, 40, 53
Menes, 13, 15, 17, 22
Menkaure, 34, 61
Mentuhotep, 40, 45
Middle Kingdom, 8, 40, 43, 47
monuments, 9, 27, 37, 40, 45, 47, 55, *60*
  inscriptions on, 55
mortuary temple, 22, 32
mummies, 7, 8, 28
mummification, 28-29
Mycerinus, 9, 34

Narmer. *See* Menes
Narmer Palette, 13
natron, 29
Nebuchadrezzar, 54
Nefertiti, 49, 50
New Kingdom, 8, 36, 43, 47, 48
Nile, 11, 22, 30, 32, 36, 39, 40, 48
  delta, 15, 20, 41, 51, 53, 54
  valley, 11, 60
  west bank, 46
nomes, 13, 17, 39

Octavian, 55
Old Kingdom, 8, 9, 15, 17, 21, 37, 39, 46, 47, 48
  characteristics of, 39, 42, 48
Opening of the Mouth, 8

Palette, Narmer, 13
Pepi I, 36
pharaoh, 7, 17, 18, 20, 21, 23, 34, 36, 39, 40, 47
  religious power of, 39, 49
  role, 17, 43

worshipped as a god, 23, 49
prayers, 32, 50
priests, 7, 17, 18, 20, 29, 31, 39, 48, 49
Ptolemy, 55
pyramid, 17, 22, 60
  complex, 22, 46
  construction, 23, 24-25, 27, 30-33
  development, 22-26
  kinds of, 17, 23, 24, 25-26, 30
  shape, 26-27
  See also building materials; quarries; tools

quarries, 30
queens, 20, 25, 46, 49, 50

Ramses II (the Great), 36, 51, 53, 60, 61
Ramses III, 20, 51
reliefs, 40
religion, ancient, 17, 19, 20, 46, 50
religious beliefs
  afterlife, 22, 51
  pharaoh, 20, 23, 49
rescue archaeology, 57, *60*, 60
Rosetta Stone, 55

Sahure, 7-9
Saqqara, 17, 22, 23, 25, 41
sarcophagus, 7, *8*, *28*, 34
Satrap, 55
science, 9, 18, 26, 31
scribes, 18, 30, 43
sculptures, 34, 49
Sekhmet, 35
Senemut, 46
Sesiotris I, *38*, 40
Seth, 19
Snefru, 24, 25, 26, 30, 32, 46
society, changes in, 36, 39, 48, 53
soil, 12, 55, 57

Sphinx, 9, 34, *35*, 36, *37*
Sphinx Temple, 36
statues, 34, 40, 47, 51, *57*
sun, 9, 19, 22, 26

taxes, 40, 55
temple, 18, 22, 32, 34, 45-46, 47, 48, 59
  complex, *45*, 47, 53
  Karnak, 39, 40, *42*, 47
texts, religious, 50, 51
Thebes, 19, 40, 42, 45, 46, 49, 53
Thutmose I, 44
Thutmose II, 44
Thutmose III, 46, *47*, 47, 48, 49
Thutmose IV, 36
tomb, 28
  pharaoh's, 7, 21, 22, 30, 40, 50
tombs, 21, 41
  decoration, 18
  nobles, 36, 50
  royal, 40, 59
tools, 7, 20, 22, 27, 30, 32
trade
  goods, 30, 40, 42
  routes, 40, 45, 48
Tutankhamen, *51*, 51, 60

underworld, 21, 22, 36
Upper Egypt, 11, 13, 36, 39, 40

Valley of the Kings, 51
valley temple, 32, 34
  See also Great Pyramid; Giza
vizier, 17, 43, 53

war, 41, 43-44, 47
women in Egyptian society, 18, 18-20
writing. *See* hieroglyphic writing
written records, 8, 18, 26, 50, 51, 59

Zoser, *16*, 23, 30 46

SUGGESTED READING

Edwards, I.E.S. *The Pyramids of Egypt*. New York: Viking, 1987.

Hobson, Christine. *The World of the Pharaohs: A Complete Guide to Ancient Egypt*. New York: Thames & Hudson, 1987.

Kamil, Jill. *The Ancient Egyptians: A Popular Introduction to Life in the Pyramid Age*. New York: Columbia University Press, 1986.

Malek, Jaromir, and Werner Forman. *In the Shadow of the Pyramids: Ancient Egypt During the Old Kingdom*. Norman, Okla.: University of Oklahoma Press, 1986.

Millard, Anne. *The Egyptians*. Englewood Cliffs, N.J.: Silver Burdett, 1977.

Pace, Mildred M. *Pyramids: Tombs for Eternity*. New York: McGraw-Hill, 1981.

Santrey, Lawrence. *Ancient Egypt*. Mahwah, N.J.: Troll Associates, 1985.

Weeks, John. *The Pyramids*. New York: Lerner Publications, 1977.

Picture Credits

About the Author

Carter Smith III is an editor and writer living in the Boston area. The author of *One Giant Leap for Mankind* in Silver Burdett Press's *Turning Points in American History* series, he is a graduate of Beloit College.

DATE DUE

DISCARDED